What's it like to be a...
POSTAL WORKER

Written by Morgan Matthews
Illustrated by Mark A. Hicks

Troll Associates

Special Consultant: Richard J. Alderman, *Postmaster, Mahwah, New Jersey.*

Library of Congress Cataloging-in-Publication Data

Matthews, Morgan.
  What's it like to be a postal worker / by Morgan Matthews;
illustrated by Mark A. Hicks.
    p.   cm.—(Young careers)
  Summary: Describes the many tasks performed by the people who keep
the mail moving in the postal service.
  ISBN 0-8167-1813-X (lib. bdg.)   ISBN 0-8167-1814-8 (pbk.)
  1. Postal service—Employees—Juvenile literature. 2. Postal
service—Vocational guidance—Juvenile literature. [1. Postal
service. 2. Occupations.] I. Hicks, Mark A., ill. II. Title.
  III. Series.
  HE6499.M17   1990
  383'.023'73—dc20   89-34385

What's it like to be a...
POSTAL WORKER

A letter goes in a mailbox. Who picks it up?
How does it get to the right place? Who delivers
the letter? Let's find out.

Many people work together to move the mail.
They are part of the postal service.

Mailbox

Automatic Stamp
Machine

UNITED STATES POST OFFICE
CORTARO, ARIZONA
85652

Most towns have their own post offices. Men
and women who work at the post office are
called postal workers—and each one has an
important job to do!

Name Tag

Counter

Some postal workers stand at windows in the post office. They help people who want to mail letters and packages. They sell stamps, post cards, and other services.

Letters need stamps to be delivered. There are many, many kinds of stamps. They come in different shapes and sizes. Some people collect postage stamps for a hobby. It can be fun!

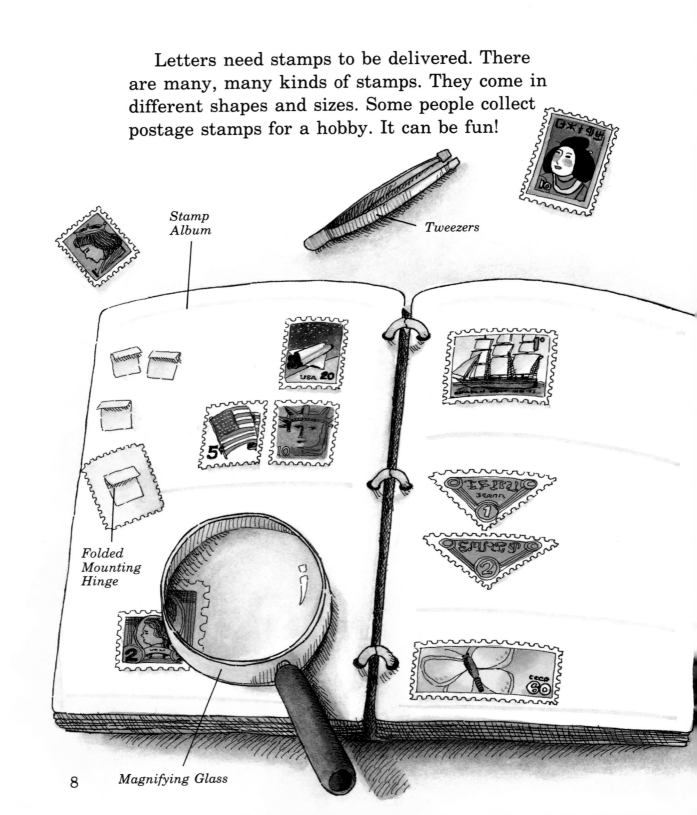

Stamp Album

Tweezers

Folded Mounting Hinge

Magnifying Glass

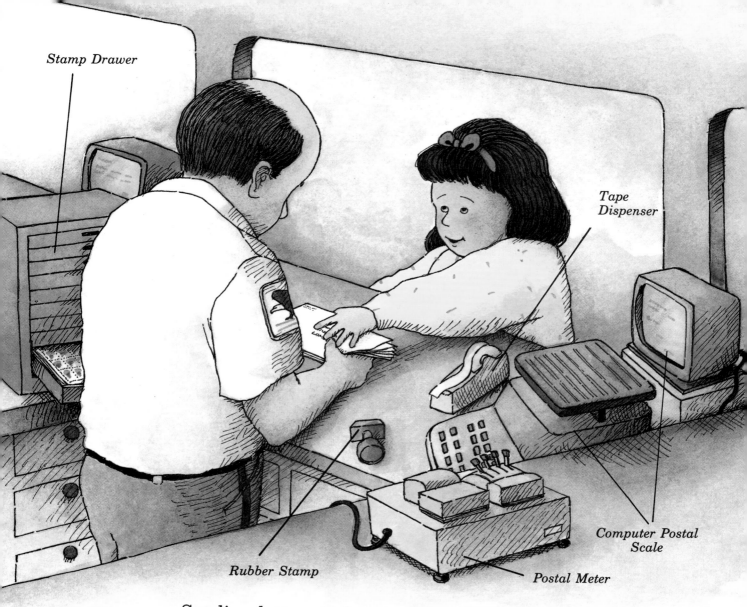

Stamp Drawer

Tape Dispenser

Computer Postal Scale

Rubber Stamp

Postal Meter

Sending letters is fun, too! Sandy mails a lot of letters to her pen pals.

"Six first-class stamps, please!" she says to the postal worker. "I have six letters to mail. And this one is going to England!"

The postal service delivers letters to places all over the world.

Into a mailbox go Sandy's letters. The letters are on their way! A letter carrier stops on his way back to the post office. He empties the box and brings the letters to the post office with him.

Time Schedule
For Mail Pickup

Mail Sack

10

Mail Sacks

Portable Bins

At the post office are piles of letters. There are packages, parcels, and bundles, too. Each one must be delivered. Now the hard work begins!

Special mail must be separated from regular mail. At small post offices, workers separate mail at a table. Big post offices use a conveyor belt.

Letters roll by. Workers separate the mail. Magazines go here. Very large envelopes go there. Sandy's letters go in a sack.

Mail Sacks

Identification
Tag

Conveyor
Belt

13

Trays

Noise Protectors

Next, the mail must be postmarked and canceled. Postal workers use special machines. They put stacks of letters into the machines.

The machine prints a postmark on each letter. It shows the date and place the letter was mailed from. The machine also cancels stamps. It prints lines on them, so they can't be used again.

Cancellation Marks

City

State

Zip Code

ALBANY NY
—
JUNE
06
—
1989

25 USA

Date

Postmark

Now the letters are ready for sorting. A special high-speed machine does the job. Skilled workers are trained to use it.

Machine Number

Postmark

Light

Zip Code Number Keys

Letter Tray

A worker sits at the machine. *Whiz!* A letter slides out from the stack. The sorter has seconds to see the zip code. She presses typewriter-like keys.

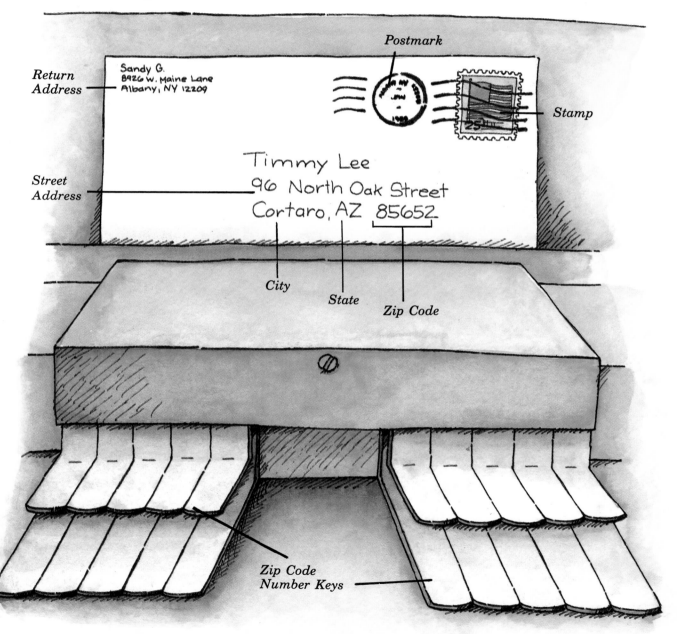

The letter goes into one of many bins behind the machine. Each of Sandy's letters goes into a different bin. Each bin has a different zip code that represents a different area.

Workers take mail out of the bins. Important items may be sent by a special service called Express Mail. "First-class" items are important, too. They travel faster than regular mail.

Mail Sack

Mail Tray

First-class letters are put in trays or sacks. Some sacks weigh seventy pounds. Postal workers must be able to lift the heavy sacks.

20

Now the mail is on its way. Day and night, postal trucks carry away mail. The trucks may drive to railroad stations and airports so the mail can travel by train or plane.

Exhaust Pipe

U.S. MAIL

U.S.MAIL

Rearview Mirror

Fuel Filler Cap

Fuel Tank

Sandy's letter to England travels by jet.
Jets fly mail to countries all over the world.
Mail also travels by jet to distant states.
When the jet lands, mail trucks are waiting.
They take the mail to a large postal center,
where workers do more sorting.

Hangars

Jet Engines

U.S. MAIL

U.S. MAIL

23

One of Sandy's letters zips past. It's on its way to a nearby post office.

Truck Number

Front
Safety
Mirror

Logo

Rural
Mailboxes

U.S. MAIL

It arrives early in the morning. A postal
worker sorts the mail for a letter carrier's route.

Each carrier has a tray filled with letters that are ready to be delivered that day. And each carrier has a special route. One of Sandy's letters is addressed to a boy on Ellen Hansen's route.

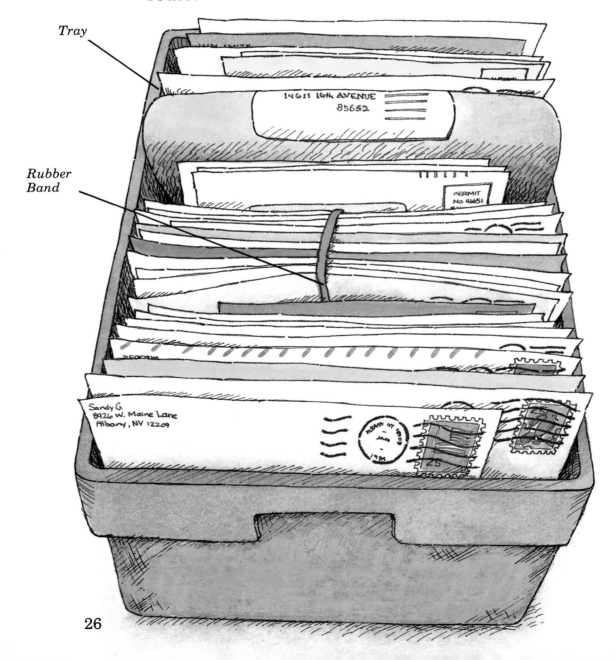

Tray

Rubber Band

Dog
Repellent

Official
Patch

Identification
Badge

Timmy Lee
North Oak Street
Cortaro, AZ 85652

U.S. MAIL

Mailbag

Ellen puts her mail in order.

"Here's a letter from Timmy's pen pal," she
says.

Ellen puts the mail in her bag.

Then she leaves the post office. Off she goes to deliver the mail. Some letter carriers do a lot of walking. Other letter carriers ride in mail trucks.

This letter carrier goes from house to house.
Timmy's house is next.

"Any mail for me?" asks Timmy.
Ellen gives him Sandy's letter. Timmy smiles
and races to his room to read it.

Timmy is a good pen pal. He writes back soon. Tomorrow, he will mail the letter to Sandy. And soon, Sandy's letter carrier will deliver the letter to her.

What do you think it will say?

Dear Sandy,

Stamp

32